PUGLIA

GATEWAY TO THE EAST

WHITE STAR PUBLISHERS

PUGLIA
GATEWAY TO THE EAST

PHOTOGRAPHS
Antonio Attini

TEXT
Carlos Solito

Contents

2-3 Bari's historic district is dominated by the massive cathedral of San Sabino (right, in the picture), built between the 12th and 13th centuries. The typical Apulian Romanesque façade is flanked by a tall campanile and the *trulla*, a circular structure that was probably a baptistery.

4-5 Puglia's flat, even Adriatic coastline changes toward the Gargano peninsula, where the mountainous terrain is covered with thick woods that reach down to the sea in some places.

6-7 The cathedral in the little Apulian town of Giovinazzo (Bari province) rises above the old fortified section, which adjoins the Old Port.

8 Punta del Grottone and the Cala Grande lighthouse on Capraia, one of the Tremiti Islands (Foggia province), lead on to Punta Secca, which extends into the cobalt blue sea.

9 The characteristic houses of Alberobello (Bari province), known as *trulli*, are believed to date from prehistoric times. The round buildings, which have square interiors, have conical roofs formed by concentric circles of stone.

Puglia is the region known as the heel of Italy, but it is also the finger that the country points eastward and the bridge that unites and rather than divides, just like the Mediterranean. Indeed, the region reaches out into the waters of this same sea, dazzled by the midday sun. It is the magic spell of a unique location, the home of the sun and the wind. The sonorous chant of one, ten, a hundred or a thousand cicadas fills your ears. The perfumes of the scrub and the salt-laden breezes tickle your nose, making you sneeze with pleasure. The ancient, rough rocks, brimming with history, graze you as you pass and beckon to be caressed. The fig, almond and pomegranate trees, prickly pears and wild vegetables are gifts to be savored each time you pause along the dusty tracks, between the slabs of hard limestone framed by carpets of fertile, iron-rich red earth, which stains your hands and is praised by the peasants. All around are dry-stone walls crawling with lizards and geckos; whitewashed *trulli*; clusters of poppies; aromatic rosemary; and the ubiquitous gnarled olive trees, cracked like fossils. Whichever border you cross to reach Puglia, you will always be greeted by an olive tree, even from above, looking down from the sky. In every single corner of the region of ancient Puglia, beloved by Frederick II of Swabia, the countryside glimmers with the silvery flash of olive groves, which have constituted its wealth for centuries.

Wise patriarch and also mother, with riches, dignity, history, love, power and determination: Puglia has multiple identities from the Gargano to the Salentine Peninsula, not forgetting the Murge. There are many Puglias, united in a single region with a particular charm of its own, which it is impossible to elude. Visiting Puglia is a journey just a stone's throw from home, a trip to an exotic location where the sea is always visible. The Adriatic and Ionian Seas lap 500 miles of coastline. This indescribable sequence of sand and bizarrely striped stratified limestone rocks forms strange lines and curves, creating symbols that fire the imagination and can be interpreted like dreams. Perhaps these symbols also attracted the attention of those who arrived from distant lands by sea, and chose this frontier region as their new home. The Messapii, Dauni and Iapyges were the first to inhabit the region after prehistoric man. They were followed by waves of Greek migrants who formed colonies that collectively became known as Magna Graecia, a thriving region of culture and industry, art and learning.

Following the decline of the Romans, who arrived in the region in the 4th century B.C. (founding *municipia* and intensifying the cultivation of cereals and the production of olive oil), during the Middle Ages the Byzantines, Lombards, Arabs, Normans and Swabians in succession dominated Apuia. During this period a cave civilization developed and austere cathedrals with outstanding sculptural decoration were built in what became known as the Apulian

10 The Alto (or Porto Selvaggio) watch tower stands on a rocky spur known as La Dannata, near Nardò (Lecce province) It was built by Alonso Salazar in 1568.

Romanesque style. At the same time, Emperor Frederick II of Swabia, "*Stupor Mundi*," erected a defensive line of massive fortified castles and manors across the region, including the extraordinary Castel del Monte, an octagonal gem of hard rock.

During the 16th century, olive cultivation was further intensified and the aristocracy, middle class and clergy planted their properties with endless olive groves and established farms on the site of ancient estates and near cave settlements (stock farms were also founded for the raising of horses, cattle, goats and pigs). Almost invariably, these had a very simple plan built around a courtyard. Following an artistic hiatus of around three centuries, the exuberant Baroque style exploded in Lecce and spread across the re-

gion to embellish the simple, unadorned façades of the medieval monuments.

Every little corner of Puglia displays a piece of history. The coasts and inland regions are brimming with the traces that humankind has left over the ages, marking a clear sequence of epochs starting with the distant Stone Age. The visitor requires plenty of time to admire the magical visions of the past; discover watchtowers and Roman, monastic and Swabian relics; pray in silent sanctuaries; visit abbeys grizzled by time; explore the Romanesque, Gothic and Baroque churches; and wander among the huge estates of the farms and the *trulli*, standing proud against the sky. A bird's-eye view of the region reveals that Puglia

12 left From north to south, Puglia is a checkerboard of farmland, dominated by olive groves and vineyards that yield world-renowned oils and wines.

can be explored by tracing dozens and dozens of itineraries from north to south. The low white hamlets are packed with cube-shaped buildings that line mazes of narrow streets, juxtaposed with churches and palaces guarded by figures from the Romanesque and Baroque bestiaries.

Outside the urban areas, the region vaunts cliffs topped with Mediterranean scrub; golden beaches fringed with Aleppo pines; the haughty limestone crags of the Gargano Peninsula, where the last great forest still survives; the fertile Puglia Tableland with its sea of wheat and rows of vines; and the rounded Daunian Pre-Apennines between Campania and Molise. Farther south is the rocky Murge plateau with its geological monuments, and the ravines of the Ionian coastal strip, which snake like long dragons between the entrances of underground caverns and spectacular caves embellished with age-old mineral deposits. The final strip of land reaching out into the sea is the Salentine Peninsula. Here the landscape is dominated by the olive, whose fleshy fruit that yields first-rate extra-virgin oil has always made it king of the countryside and a goldmine for the local people. Puglia abruptly ends at Santa Maria di Leuca, amid Mediterranean perfumes to be savored

in the shade of a Saracen tower or a fin-de-siècle villa. Then there's Bari, the regional capital, and Brindisi, Foggia, Lecce and Taranto, where the sea, land and wind seem to be embodied in the architecture, creating a carefully calibrated urban synthesis of the pivotal elements of a region that deserves to be experienced in every way.

Our trip above Puglia will feature three itineraries. The first will take us over the cities, towns and villages, allowing us to admire historical and cultural gems of which the region is rightly proud. The second is a journey above the extraordinary deep blue sea – or rather seas, for there are two of them – in search of evocative sights. The Adriatic and Ionian Seas seem to caress, buffet and overflow into each other, with their crystal-clear waters, breaking surf, melodious roar and raging walls of water. These two seas have carved the region's coasts, tracing lines and curves, sketching cliffs, zigzagging bays and drawing long straight beaches. They erode the rocks, transforming them into mere pebbles and sand that they scatter at whim, and intensify the blackness of the entrances of the marine grottoes before diluting it with strokes of turquoise and blinding sunlight. In short, they have always amused

12 center Just north of Otranto (Lecce province), the coast forms a series of little rocky bays lapped by crystal-clear waters. They are backed by scrubland crisscrossed with paths trodden by the many bathers and naturalists who frequent the area.

12 right Barletta, with its many historic monuments, Andria and Trani have merged to form the new province of Barletta-Andria-Trani, the first in Italy to be headed by three cities.

themselves by changing the geography of the region, arbitrarily and without rules comprehensible to humankind, following a method peculiar to nature. They have made a masterly job of it, judging by the results, yet they continue their ongoing labor unnoticed by single generations. This succession of glimmering waters and coasts is an evocative sight, with surprising colors and light that have always attracted colonists and enchanted wayfarers, pilgrims, saints, Crusaders, painters and writers, who have entrusted their intimate emotions to words. "Flaming red walls erected by the gods to guard a paradise" is how Ferdinand Gregorovius described a sunset over the rocks of the Gargano Peninsula. After hunting near the salt marshes of Margherita di Savoia, Frederick II, Duke of Swabia wrote, "If the Lord had known this plain of Puglia, light of my eyes, he would have stopped to dwell here." Tommaso Fiore described the Adriatic with the following words, "the deep blue and purple hues of the sea, and here and there the countless villages stretching out like white strips. . . ." In his Odes, the Roman poet Horace referred to his beloved Galesus River on the Ionian coast, "that corner of the world smiles in my eye beyond all others. . . ."

However, Puglia is not only endless expanses of sea, but also a sweeping extent of land. The third itinerary above the region reveals the best of this inland area, which unfurls like a carpet beyond the coastline. This is the heart of Puglia, which faces away from the Adriatic and Ionian Seas. It is a relatively flat region of plains and hills, where mountainous terrain accounts for just 2 percent of the total area. Indeed, Puglia is the Italian region with the fewest mountains and consequently has a low average altitude. While this may conjure up images of a world with an unchanging horizon in all directions, Puglia actually boasts an incredible array of landscapes. The region offers a huge variety of scenery, with majestic natural views, where timid mountains fall sheer to form canyons and extend arms of land into valleys, which proudly open into plains and salt marshes. This dizzy effect of movement is repeated with the Murge plateau and ravines, which are followed by more plains, carpeted with an unbroken expanse of olive trees.

Puglia is an ideal region for touring by bicycle or car, on foot or on horseback, by sailboat or by rubber dinghy. Better still, by paraglider or hang glider, to admire it from above, taking it in at a glance and grasping the structure, history and nature of land that is basically flat, but has as many facets as the most precious diamond. Happy flying over the kaleidoscopic world of Puglia!

15 The little town of Peschici (Foggia province) with its maze of narrow streets and small squares is perched atop a high limestone cliff overlooking the Adriatic Sea. The 11th-century castle is one of its most prominent landmarks.

Basic Information about Puglia region

- Area: 7476 sq. miles (19,362 sq. km)
- Population: 4,023,957 (latest census)
- Regional capital: Bari (315,068 inhabitants)
- Provincial capitals: Barletta (92,436 inhabitants), Andria (96,311), Trani (53,345); Brindisi (88,536), Foggia (154,970), Lecce (83,923), Taranto (200,436).
- The territory is 53.2% flatlands and plains, 45.3% hilly, and 1.5% mountainous.
- Main rivers: Puglia's main rivers are seasonal and include the Candelaro, the Cervaro and the Carapelle, although several larger ones, such as the Ofanto and the Fortore, flow through part of Puglia.
- Main lakes: the largest lakes are Lesina and Varano in the Gargano Peninsula in the northeastern Puglia. The Otranto area of the Salentine Peninsula, in the southeast, is home to the Alimini Lakes, while the little Cillarese Lake is situated near Brindisi.
- Main islands: the main islands are the Tremiti group with an area of 1.21 sq. miles/(3.1 sq. km and 420 permanent inhabitants, which comprises San Domino, San Nicola, Capraia, Pianosa and Cretaccio.
- Puglia is divided into 258 municipalities.
- Population density: 645 per sq. mile (248 per sq. km).
- Nature reserves in Puglia: Alta Murgia National Park, Gargano National Park, Otranto Coast, Santa Maria di Leuca and Tricase Forest Regional Park, Lama Balice Regional Park, Torre Canne-Torre San Leonardo Coastal Dunes Regional Park, Punta della Contessa Saltpan Regional Park, Porto Selvaggio-Torre Uluzzo Regional Park.

16 Puglia forms the southeastern tip of peninsular Italy. Its position as a bridge toward Greece and the Middle East is particularly clear in this satellite picture, which is slightly distorted by the curvature of the Earth.

18-19 Farther west, the Murgia di Locorotondo (province of Bari) slopes gently toward the Adriatic Sea, covered with a checkerboard of olive groves, vineyards and orchards crossed by dusty white tracks leading to huge farms.

20-21 Lecce's Roman amphitheater (dating from about the 2nd century A.D.) occupies most of Piazza Sant'Oronzo; it is one of the city's best-preserved Roman buildings.

22-23 The municipal territory of Altamura (Bari province) covers many square miles in the northwest part of the Murge plateau, characterized by vast pastures and numerous farmhouses, *trulli* and sheep pens *(jazzi)*.

TOWNS AND CITIES

Puglia is almost completely flat, making it ideal for the construction of towns and cities. Bari is the first stop on the itinerary for those wishing to discover the region's urban face. It is a city with two distinct sides: old and new, embodied in the medieval historic district and the modern Murattiano quarter. However, faith and piety are also a fundamental part of its character. Indeed, Bari is identified with St Nicholas, the world's best-known saint and the city's patron since 1087, when local sailors abducted his relics from Myra, in Asia Minor, and brought them back to their hometown. Here they are venerated in a procession on May 7, 8 and 9 each year, attracting thousands of people from as far away as Russia. The event offers an excellent opportunity to explore the city, starting from the old port and continuing to the medieval quarter, dominated by the cathedral of San Sabino, built in 1170. Nearby, the picturesque old city is the site of the basilica of San Nicola, a gem of Apulian Romanesque architecture, which houses the relics of Saint Nicholas, the 12th-century marble cathedra of Bishop Elias, and a fine sculpted ciborium. The Norman castle, built by Frederick II, is equally imposing, while the Murattiano district is a triumph of Neoclassical and Art Nouveau buildings, monuments from the Fascist period and theaters, of which the Petruzzelli is the finest example.

The area around Bari – part of which has recently been incorporated into the new province of Barletta-Andria-Trani – comprises several attractive towns, such as Bitonto, a famous center of olive oil production along the Via Traiana, which boasts a handsome Romanesque cathedral facing the Baroque obelisk dedicated to the Immaculate Conception. The nearby town of Ruvo di Puglia has a fine Romanesque cathedral with several Gothic features, decorated with lions and griffins, and Altamura is home to another a great cathedral, commissioned by Frederick II. The picturesque Fondovico district of the town of Gravina in Puglia, on the border with Basilicata, is perched above a ravine, while the Scesciola quarter of Minervino Murge overlooks the Ofanto and Bradano river valleys from an enchanting panoramic position. Canosa di Puglia is also scenically located and vaunts the fine episcopal cathedral of San Sabino and the archaeological site of ancient Cannae.

24 left San Foca, a hamlet of Melendugno (Lecce province) is situated near Otranto on the coast between San Cataldo and Santa Maria di Leuca. It is a popular seaside resort renowned for its sandy coves.

24 right The church of San Martino in Martina Franca (Taranto province), known locally as the *collegiata*, was built between 1747 and 1763 on the foundations of a Romanesque church.

25 Flying over the historic district of Bari (Barivecchia) is like looking down on an intricate spider's web. The limestone-paved streets widen into squares and little piazzas, before narrowing again to wind between white houses, passing the city's most illustrious monuments.

27 Molfetta (Bari province) is one of Puglia's most active fishing towns. Its stone historic district is situated next to the port, overlooking the Adriatic Sea.

The province of Foggia lies on the far side of the Ofanto River. Cerignola, set among the olive groves, is announced by the huge dome of its cathedral, which is particularly visible from above. The Puglia Tableland is home to Lucera – a former Roman *municipium*, as testified by its amphitheater – whose huge castle on top of the Albano hill is a blend of Roman, Norman and Angevin architecture. The Daunian Pre-Apennines are dotted with a string of little stone villages with pitched roofs dominated by medieval towers, castles and churches. Ascoli Satriano, Biccari, Bovino, Celenza Valfortore, Deliceto, Faeto, Monteleone di Puglia, Orsara di Puglia and Rocchetta Sant'Antonio all have breathtaking settings. This area of Puglia resembles the Irpinia region of Campania, with the exception of Troia, a little town whose basilica is a Romanesque gem incorporating Arab and Byzantine features and a stunning rose window. Foggia was a favorite city of Frederick II. A series of earthquakes have destroyed much of its original structure, leaving it with fewer monuments than the other main cities of the region. Piazza De Sanctis and its Apulian Romanesque cathedral are the first sights on a tour of the city that commences near the fountain and Via Arpi, which leads to the Porta Grande. Nearby, beyond the Three Arches, stands the Epitaffio obelisk, the church of San Giovanni Battista, the church of the Columns and the church of the Crosses, which features a triumphal arch and five chapels.

On the opposite side, to the east, the main town of the Gargano Peninsula is Monte Sant'Angelo, with the terraced houses of the Jun-

28 left The old town of Monopoli, on the Adriatic coast, is protected by a wall with ramparts built during the 15th century by Don Pedro of Toledo, Viceroy of Naples, to guard it against attacks from the sea. Its bastions (named Madonna, Re Ferrante, Santa Maria, Portavecchia, Batteria, Cavaliere, Portavecchia, Massercola, Molini and Papacenere) acted as lookout points from which the sea was scanned in all directions and from which assaults were prepared.

no quarter, the ubiquitous castle built by Frederick II and the sanctuary of San Michele Arcangelo, with its octagonal tower and grotto packed with pilgrims. Pilgrims also flock to the Padre Pio Pilgrimage Church in San Giovanni Rotondo and to the sanctuary of San Matteo in San Marco in Lamis, surrounded by shady forests. The ancient towns of Sannicandro, Carpino and Vico del Gargano nestle on the gentle slopes, as though painted by a great master capable of blending the light and colors of the stone with the silver of the olive groves and the orange of the famous Gargano oranges in a few brushstrokes.

South of Bari, the Bassa Murgia (Lower Murgia) is dotted with trulli, the conical, stone-roofed buildings of the region. In Alberobello the trulli are clustered on the slopes of the Monti and Aia Piccola quarters, which UNESCO has designated as a World Heritage Site. From above, this is the most beautiful village in Puglia, with little pyramids topped with decorative pinnacles and adorned with sacred and secular symbols. Locorotondo, Cisternino and particularly Martina Franca in the Itria Valley are equally dazzling. A veritable procession of façades and details of important monuments unfurls in the latter: the Ducal Palace, the collegiate church of San Martino, the church of the Carmine and Via Principe Umberto with its sumptuous palaces. Another town not to be missed is Ceglie Messapica, with its majestic castle above the square with the clock tower, while Grottaglie – surrounded by deep ravines like Massafra, Mottola, Castellaneta, Laterza and Ginosa – has an ancient potters' quarter, churches, convents and a historic district that attracts crowds of tourists.

Nearby is Taranto, founded as Taras by Greek settlers from Sparta. All that now remains of the ancient city are its treasures on display in the national archaeological museum and the columns of the Doric Temple of Poseidon, dating from the 6th century B.C. Highlights of Taranto include its Baroque and Art Nouveau buildings, the garden of Villa Garibaldi, Piazza Vittoria and Piazza Maria Immacolata. Beyond the swing bridge, the old city is dominated by the circular Aragonese castle, whose earliest nucleus dates from the 10th century. The historic district is home to important monuments and the cathedral of San Cataldo alone – like the sumptuously decorated Baroque chapel of the same name – is worth a visit.

Southern Puglia's greatest example of military architecture can be admired in Oria, on the Messapian plain. This fortress, rebuilt by Frederick II with towers and battlements, offers views for miles around. Nearby are Manduria, with its Messapian necropolis cut out of the rock, and Brindisi, sandwiched between the natural inlets of

28 center Porto Cesareo, north of Gallipoli, boasts crystal-clear sea, whose transparency rivals that of the tropics. A stroll along the sandy beach overlooking Conigli island and the other atolls conveys the intimate soul of the town that has developed around a picturesque little port.

28 right Oria cathedral (in Brindisi province) was rebuilt in 1756 with a Baroque façade flanked by a clock tower and dominated by a tiled dome.

the Seno di Levante and Seno di Ponente and the island of San-t'Andrea. The two Roman columns marking the end of the Appian Way stand on the seashore, while the city center is home to the newly restored cathedral, the provincial archaeological museum and the Romanesque churches of Santa Lucia, San Benedetto and San Giovanni al Sepolcro, built by the Knights Templar. Outside the city is the church of Santa Maria al Casale, richly decorated with 14th-century frescoes.

Lecce is a breathtaking mosaic of Baroque wonders, brimming with churches and palaces whose façades are adorned with arches, portals and balconies and decorated with tracery, columns, saints, floral sprays and fantastic figures. The Porta Rudiae or the Porta Napoli are the best entrances to this spectacular city, as they are followed by a dizzy sequence of monuments: the 18th-century church of the Rosario, Palazzo Lecciso, Piazza Duomo with the cathedral with tall campanile, the church of Santa Maria Assunta and the Bishops' Palace, The rusticated stonework of the Celestine monastery contrasts with the impossibly ornate façade of the basilica of Santa Croce, with its petrified flights of fancy crowded with garlands and festoons, caryatids and cherubs, flowers and fruit, flourishes and bestiaries, saints and capitals. The city's main meeting place is Piazza Sant'Oronzo, which is home to a 2nd-century Roman amphitheater and the column of Sant'Oronzo. Below Lecce, the towns of Monteroni, Copertino and Cavallino – home respectively to the ducal palace, castle and Palazzo Castromediano – are set among vineyards planted with the Negroamaro grapes used to produce the heady Salice Salentino wine. Acaja is also home to a fortress, or rather a fortified citadel.

Grecia Salentina constitutes an island within the peninsula. This cluster of villages shares a Greek dialect and the *pizzica*, an almost hysterical dance long believed to be the only cure for the venomous bite of the wolf spider. Corigliano d'Otranto and the Castello de' Monti, Soleto and the daring Raimondello campanile, Galatone and the church of the Crocefisso are just a few of the highlights. However, the greatest attraction is Galatina, with the church of Santa Caterina d'Alessandria boasting a gallery with 15th-century frescoes by masters of the Marche and Emilia schools. Nardò is equally impressive, with the elaborate façade of the church of San Domenico, the octagonal shrine in Piazza Osanna and the central Piazza Salandra around the Immacolata column. Several miles farther south, the little town of Muro Leccese is home to the Rococo-style churches of Santa Maria Annunziata and Santa Maria Immacolata, while Casaranello boasts the Byzantine church of Santa Maria della Croce, which houses an Early Christian mosaic dating from the 5th century.

31 It is worth visiting the Salentine Peninsula for Gallipoli (Lecce province) alone. Situated on the Ionian coast, the town boasts many artistic and historical treasures, and it comes as no surprise to learn that the ancient Greek settlers called it Kalépólis, "Beautiful City." Each summer the town and its surrounding beaches are invaded by thousands of tourists.

32 The historic district of Bari extends toward the new port, flanked by the massive castle built by Frederick II.

33 left In 1991 a fire bomb devastated the interior of Bari's Petruzzelli theater, one of the grandest opera houses in Italy and the symbol of the city's cultural life.

33 right The dual architectural identity of Bari Castle is immediately apparent from above. The first, innermost, one was built during Hohenstaufen rule, between 1230 and 1250, while the second was built by the Aragonese with angular bastions.

34 The Rotonda, Nazario Sauro and Crollalanza esplanades can be seen in this view, along with the old port, from which the fishermen still set sail each day.

35 The campanile of the cathedral of San Sabino rises above the white cubic buildings of Barivecchia, seeming to compete with the Semaforo and Minorenni towers of the castle.

36 Corso Vittorio Emanuele divides Barivecchia from the Murattiano district. The Politeama Margherita theater stands at the end of the street next to the Old Port. This Art Nouveau gem was built in 1914 and immediately became the favorite venue for variety shows and *café chantant*.

37 Three important monuments stand next to each other on the Crollalanza esplanade in Bari: the Petruzzelli theater, the Banca d'Italia building and the Chamber of Commerce (left to right).

38 Bari's Old Cathedral was built in the 11th and 12th centuries and is one of the most interesting examples of the Apulian Romanesque style. The Norman-Hohenstaufen Castle, built around 1131, is visible in the background.

39 The façade of the basilica of San Nicola in Bari displays the key features of the Apulian Romanesque style, with smooth walls interrupted by pilasters, lancet windows and three portals.

40 The Imperatore Augusto esplanade runs along the seafront of the eastern part of Barivecchia. The walls that once surrounded the entire city are still clearly visible. They were strengthened by bastions and fortifications like the 16th-century fort of Sant'Antonio that can be seen on the lower left.

41 left Just beyond Bari's Politeama Margherita theater, the Crollalanza esplanade is lined with trees, palms and elegant buildings that continue to the Nazario Sauro esplanade.

41 right The Imperatore Augusto esplanade follows the medieval walls, beyond which the basilica of San Nicola can be seen.

42 left The grounds of Lecce's monumental Villa Comunale, completed at the end of the 19th century, include corners of the Salentine countryside with avenues, ornamental plants and stone busts of illustrious local citizens.

42 right Piazza Duomo in Lecce is a sublime example of the local Baroque style. The tall campanile, and the duomo are dazzling monuments. Proceeding clockwise direction around the square, are the Bishops' Palace (1632) and the Seminary.

43 Piazza Mazzini, which hosted the 1956 International Eucharistic Congress, is Lecce's cultural rendezvous, which was laid out with trees and a central monumental fountain during the 20th-century expansion of the city.

44 Lecce is the capital of the Salentine Peninsula. Its walls enclose winding streets and little squares, shaded by palm trees. The city's many fine Baroque buildings attract hordes of tourists.

45 Lecce's Baroque center dates from the 16th and 17th centuries and commences in Piazza Sant'Oronzo (bottom right). Nearby is the oval Roman amphitheater, which could hold about 20,000 spectators. It was discovered at the beginning of the 20th century and has been partially excavated.

46-47 Even from above, Lecce is characterized by the distinctive yellow hue of the local stone. In every corner of the city this unmistakable material is exuberantly carved to form a wealth of beautiful monuments, earning the city the nickname of "Florence of the South."

48 Porta Napoli is certainly the most ostentatious of Lecce's old city gates. It takes the form of a triumphal arch, surmounted by a low-relief with a two-headed eagle, which allows access to Via Palmieri and Via Principe di Savoia.

49 The 16th-century castle of Charles V, near centrally located Piazza Sant'Oronzo, has a square plan with angular bastions and is one of Lecce's most imposing monuments.

50 left and 51 The city of Brindisi developed around a strategically situated natural port to whose shape its Roman name, Brundisium, refers. Indeed, the port is the city's lifeblood. Following its glorious classical period and medieval adventures, the port of Brindisi returned to favor during the second half of the 19th century, when it became an important terminal for shipping associated with the Dutch and British East India Companies. The port played an active role in World War I, and later in the 20th century Vittorio Emanuelle III made it the temporary capital of Italy (1943–1944).

50 right Today the port of Brindisi is an important ferry terminal for traffic to Greece and is divided into the Seno di Levane and Seno di Ponente, which meet in the Pigonati channel, guarded by the Aragonese castle (1445) on the natural island of Sant'Andrea.

52 The historic district of Taranto stands on a small island connected to the mainland by a swing bridge. Here, the city has retained its original identity, characterized by important monuments, such as the cathedral of San Cataldo, the castle and the intricate maze of narrow streets and houses.

53 Taranto's historic center is also guarded by a fortress known as the Aragonese castle (or Castel Sant'Angelo). Although founded in the 10th century, the castle was rebuilt during Aragonese, rule with a rectangular plan featuring large circular towers at each corner to withstand the attacks of the Turks.

54 Tree-lined Corso Garibaldi is home to Foggia's massive town hall, built during the Fascist period, like the Prefecture building. It is preceded by a wide flight of steps that lead to a large courtyard.

55 The flatness of the Apulian Tableland is interrupted by the bristling forest of buildings of Foggia, the capital of the old province of Capitanata. The city's historic district extends along the old Via Arpi, Piazza del Lago and Piazza De Sanctis, which is dominated by the cathedral originally built in Romanesque style.

56 and 57 Lesina lies on the Apulian Tableland, west of the lake of the same name, and can be the first or last stop on a round tour of the Gargano peninsula, the spur of the heel of Italy. Tourist attractions include the parish church, the visitors' center of the national park and La Casa del Pescatore ("Fisherman's House") museum, which houses equipment and nets that were used in ancient fishing. However, the town also has a pleasant promenade along the lake shore.

58-59 The dazzling little houses of the historic district of Peschici (Foggia province) resemble rocks protruding from the white cliff that falls sheer to the Adriatic Sea, on which the town is perfectly camouflaged. Peschici is one of the most exclusive spots of the Gargano peninsula and still boasts unspoiled Mediterranean corners, despite the devastating fires of recent years.

60 left and right The headland of Punta San Francesco forms the far eastern corner of Vieste (Foggia province) and offers fine views of picturesque Piazzetta le Ripe and the quarter of the same name. The white limestone cliffs of the little promontory are riddled with many caves and dominated by the church and *trabucco* of San Francesco.

61 The capital of the Gargano peninsula is Vieste, whose white houses and enchanting coasts have become the exclusive summer haunts of movie stars and show-business celebrities, attracted by the annual film festival.

62 San Giovanni Rotondo, which once had only a Capuchin monastery, now boasts the great church of Santa Maria delle Grazie and the recently completed Padre Pio Pilgrimage Church, by architect Renzo Piano. It attracts pilgrims from all over the world who come to pay tribute to Saint Pio of Pietralcina, canonized by Pope John Paul II on June 16, 2002.

63 The pilgrims who flock to the town where Saint Pio lived for 50 years take a tour that starts at the Capuchin monastery and proceeds to the old church, built in 1540, where the saint received the stigmata. They then visit the adjoining church of Santa Maria delle Grazie, the Casa Sollievo della Sofferenza hospital and the monumental Way of the Cross, which runs along an avenue marked with 14 bronze stations.

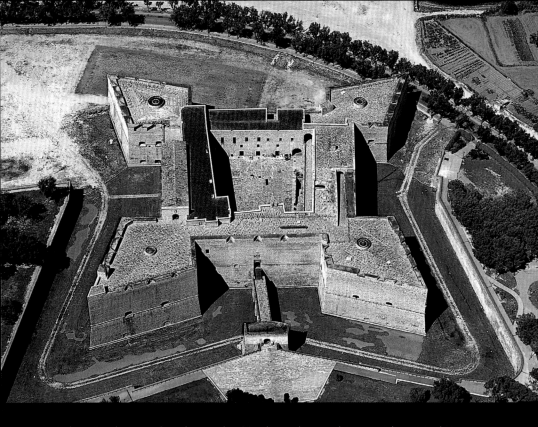

64 Barletta Castle is a colossal example of Puglia's military architecture. The original Norman building was expanded under Hohenstaufen and Aragonese rule, and again in the 16th century, when the angular bastions were added.

65 Barletta is home to the Romanesque cathedral of Santa Maria Maggiore, dating from the 12th century. The building overlooks a small square that does not allow a full appreciation of its majesty, which only becomes apparent from above, along with interesting details like the conical roofs and the campanile.

66 Trani cathedral stands near the mid-13th-century castle built by Frederick II, an example of Swabian defensive architecture that has survived largely unaltered.

67 The cathedral of San Nicola Pellegrino is Trani's main monument. It was built in the finest Apulian Romanesque style in the 11th century, uniting three churches, one on top of each other. The light-colored façade, preceded by a flight of steps, changes hue at different times of day, flushing deep red at sunset. This unusual building has a remarkable campanile and a finely carved portal.

68-69 The medieval historic district of Terlizzi (Bari province), with its dark streets and houses with blind walls, is graced by a piazza with the huge church of the Santissimo Rosario, built on the ruins of the old cathedral.

70-71 Giovinazzo (Bari province) was a fortified Roman town known as Natiolum. During its history its commercial port enabled it to establish particularly close trading connections with Venice (in the 15th century). The city is also famous for the cathedral of Santa Maria Assunta (12th-13th centuries) and the ducal palace (17th century).

72 left The old town of Giovinazzo also overlooks the sea. To defend themselves against the raids of the Turks, its inhabitants built their sturdy stone houses to form a solid wall, creating a maze of narrow streets around the old port.

72 right Piazza Vittorio Emanuele is the heart of Giovinazzo. In its center stands the monumental fountain built in 1933 by Tommaso Pisicitelli, overlooked by the former Dominican monastery with the church of San Domenico.

73 The town of Giovinazzo, just north of Bari, has ancient origins. It was founded by the Peuceti on the promontory where the historic district now stands.

74 The Romanesque cathedral of Santa Maria Assunta in Altamura (Bari province) has strong Gothic influences and can be seen for miles around. It is one of the few religious buildings commissioned by Frederick II and boasts a monumental façade between two massive bell towers and a finely carved portal guarded by a pair of austere lions.

75 Surrounded by flat stony land, the large town of Altamura breaks the monotonous landscape of the Alta Murgia. Its heart is a triumph of stone, interspersed with narrow streets and little squares.

76 and 77 Mola di Bari, just south of the regional capital, is the home of the Cima di Mola olive and a thriving agricultural and fishing center. The historic center unfolds toward the Adriatic Sea beyond Piazza XX Settembre with its monumental fountain, in a jumble of white cubes dominated by the Apulian Romanesque cathedral of San Nicola and the Angevin castle.

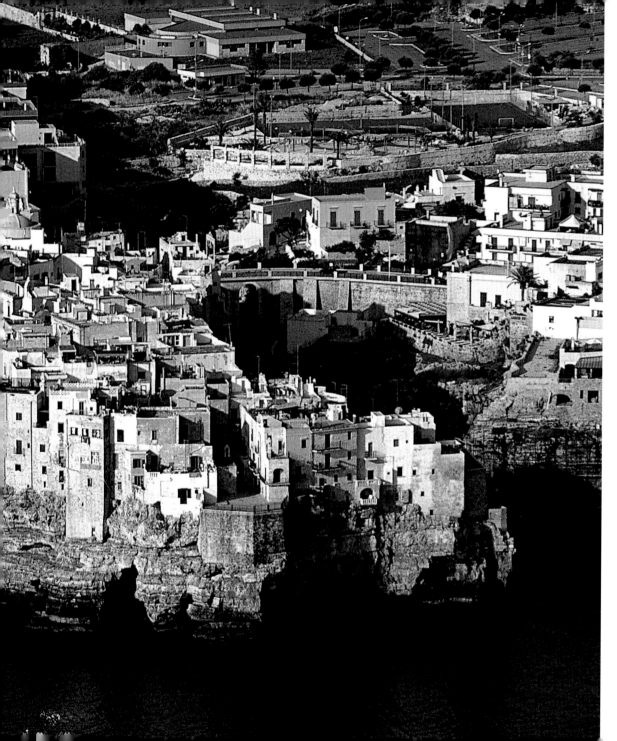

78-79 The charming historic district of Polignano a Mare (Bari province) stands on a little limestone headland riddled with marine grottoes overlooking the Adriatic Sea.

80 Founded by Greek colonists, Polignano a Mare boasts a remarkably well-preserved historic district, whose narrow streets are lined with whitewashed houses and terraces built directly above the sea. The rock below contains several well-known marine grottoes, such as the huge Palazzese cave, where the light is reflected off the water to form turquoise hues.

81 Polignano a Mare (province of Bari) is said to have been founded in the 4th century B.C. by Dionysius II of Syracuse, although excavations have revealed Neolithic traces. The church in the center is the cathedral of Santa Maria Assunta.

82-83 Monopoli, south of Bari, has long been one of Puglia's most prosperous coastal towns due to its strategic position. Its historic district is a maze of narrow streets that wind between important monuments such as the castle, Palazzo Palmieri and the church of Santa Teresa.

84 and 85 The old town of Monopoli (Bari province) is built on a roughly triangular headland dotted with some of the finest and most unusual monuments in the whole of Puglia. Highlights include the palaces of several noble families, such as Palazzo Palmieri and Palazzo Martinelli-Meo Evoli, the Baroque cathedral and many churches, including the 12th-century Santa Maria degli Amalfitani, Santa Teresa and the rock church of Madonna del Soccorso.

86 Alberobello (Bari province) is a forest of *trulli*. It is told that these unique buildings originated as a ploy by the Count of Conversano, Giangirolamo II Acquaviva of Aragon, to avoid paying taxes to the king. They are built from pieces of limestone placed on top of each other to form a series of concentric circles, and are an excellent example of natural insulation, staying cool in summer and warm in winter.

87 The bell towers of the 17th-century sanctuary of Santi Medici Cosma e Damiano, preceded by a steep flight of steps, rise above the 1500 *trulli* of Alberobello.

88 Locorotondo (Bari province) is one of the picturesque towns of the Itria Valley, which has become a famous holiday destination for international celebrities who have bought up many *trulli* and luxurious farmhouses. The white houses of the town center with their gray limestone roofs are dominated by the dome and campanile of the church of San Giorgio.

89 Conversano, southwest of Bari, was founded by the Peuceti as Norba, as revealed by the polygonal masonry walls dating from the 4th and 3rd centuries B.C. and many tombs. The historic district is a well-preserved medieval village with a Norman castle, a 13th-century cathedral built in Late Romanesque style, and a Benedictine monastery.

90 The finest of Martina Franca's monuments is the collegiate church of San Martino. It is situated in picturesque Piazza Plebiscito at the end of busy Via Vittorio Emanuele. Its façade represents the highest expression of the local Baroque style.

91 Martina Franca is undoubtedly the most picturesque town of the province of Taranto, due to the many monuments of its large historic district, built in the local Baroque style that flourished during the 18th century.

93 Ostuni, just north of Brindisi, is known as the "White Town." The reason is immediately clear: The hilltop on which it stands is a jumble of dazzling white cubic houses, which form a picturesque maze of narrow streets and steps reaching to the foot of the walls, strengthened by the Aragonese in the 16th century.

94 Piazza della Libertà stands in the heart of Ostuni. It is home to the 19th-century town hall and the Baroque obelisk of Sant'Oronzo, erected in the 18th century, in front of which the local people make the sign of the cross.

95 Giuseppe Greco's obelisk of Sant'Oronzo (1771) rises above the jumble of the distinctive white terraced houses of Ostuni (Brindisi province).

96 Otranto (Lecce province) is considered the most enchanting medieval town of the heel of Italy. The heart of its historic district is the cathedral, which boasts the largest mosaic in Europe, made by the monk Pantaleon between 1163 and 1165.

97 Otranto is one of Italy's most charming coastal towns. Its picturesque historic district is a maze of narrow stone-paved streets lined with cafés and little shops, which it is a delight to follow until reaching the panoramic viewpoints overlooking the sea. Among the white houses, walls and fortifications, rise important monuments, such as the Alfonsina tower, the castle, the Byzantine church of San Pietro and the cathedral, built in Romanesque and Gothic style with clear oriental influences, which boasts a splendid rose window.

98-99 Castro Marina (Lecce province) overlooks the blue Adriatic Sea from atop a terraced hill. The houses of the old town are dominated by a castle built in 1572 on the ruins of the old Roman fortress, which was also used by the Byzantines.

100 and 101 All the little towns of the Salentine Peninsula have white houses that shine in the sun and resemble the beads of an endless rosary when viewed from above. Castro Marina (Lecce province), with its fine monuments, clear sea and Zinzulusa cave, is one of the most popular resorts among the holidaymakers who flock to the region each summer.

102-103 Santa Maria di Leuca (Lecce province) is home to Marina del Capo, the southernmost tip of Puglia, where life seaside living has always been a tradition. The white houses alternate with the sumptuous homes of the Salentine nobility, built in Gothic Revival, Art Nouveau, Moorish and Oriental styles, such as Villa Meridiana, Villa Daniele and Villa Mellacqua.

104-105 The historic district of Gallipoli (Lecce province) is situated on a little island connected to the rest of the town by a bridge and is home to palaces with Oriental-style gardens, Baroque churches, such as that of the Purità, and the cathedral of Sant'Agata, whose magnificent interior is decorated with paintings by local and Neapolitan artists. Other highlights of the town include the Riviera Armando Diaz and Riviera Nazario Sauro esplanades that run around the base of the walls overlooking the sea; the Hellenistic fountain, dating from the 3rd century B.C.; the fishing port; and the underground olive mills, built during the 18th and 19th centuries.

LANDSCAPES

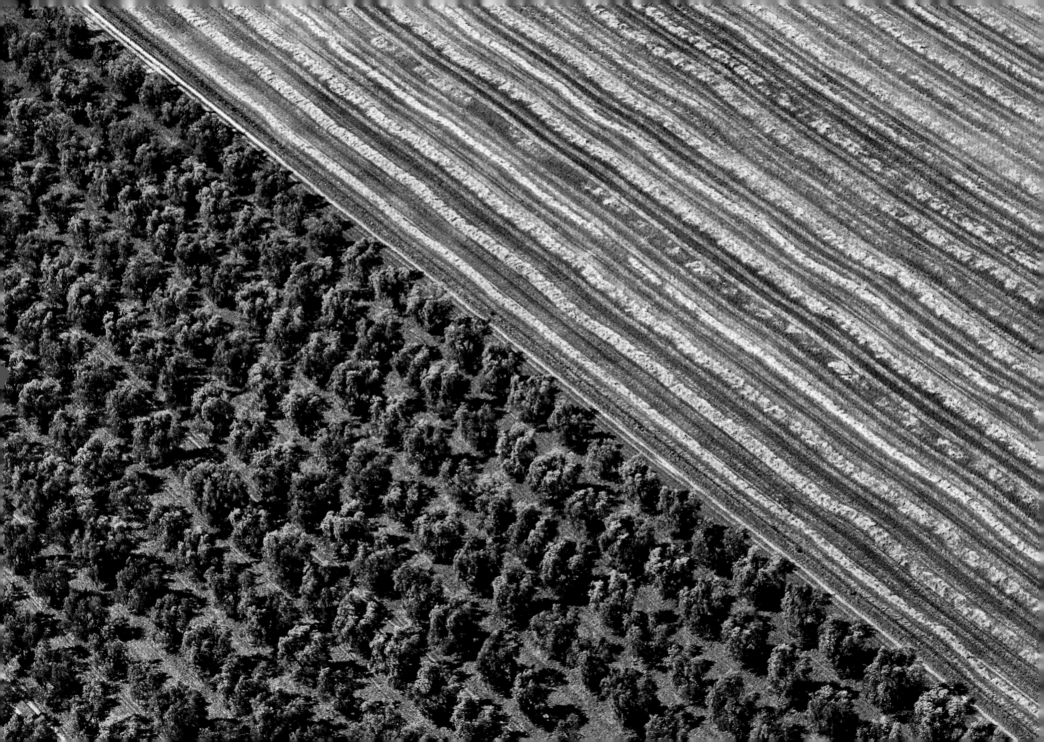

A pleasant pastime in inland Puglia is to choose a road that takes your fancy – without knowing where it leads – and to lose yourself, leaving discoveries beneath the blue sky and baking sun to chance. It is a joy to explore at whim, seeking alternative roads or rough tracks before returning to your departure point, laden with emotions, vestiges of the past, images of landscapes and scenery, agricultural knowledge, pastoral languages and magical folklore, all plucked like fruit from the trees.

Our journey commences above the Puglia Tableland, the largest plain in central and southern Italy, which covers an area of approximately 1150 sq. miles (2978 sq. km). Wheat fields extend as far as the eye can see, turning from green to yellow to brown faster than the seasons in these endless manmade grasslands created by fierce deforestation to allow intensive sheep farming. The Tableland has always been the realm of sheep, where countless flocks arrived along the age-old tracks that led down from the great mountains of Molise and Abruzzo into sunny, humid Puglia, where they sought the shade of the few scattered trees. Today the only

remnants of the old woodland are the oaks of the forest of the Incoronata. Here and there, a rare olive tree offers shade for thinking and recalling memories of fiefs, transhumance and farms that have long merged with a natural landscape tamed by extensive drainage works. It is a fertile land, planted with cereal and vegetable crops and vineyards among the drainage canals, network of roads and tracks, abandoned farmhouses and widely spaced large towns. Travel here conjures up vague images of lunar exploration, for the expanses between the settlements are deserts of silence and light. However, they are dotted with ancient relics, such as the marble ruins of the Roman city of Herdoniae; the bridge of Ascoli Satriano crossed by the army led by Pyrrhus, which defeated the troops of Publius Sulpicius Saverrio and Publius Decius Mus in 279 B.C. at the Battle of Asculum; and the crumbled stones of Castel Fiorentino, where Frederick II died on 13 December 1250, as the astrologer Michael Scot had predicted.

Then there's Passo di Corvo, the largest Neolithic village in Europe, which was discovered in 1948 by a Royal Air Force officer dur-

106 left and 107 Puglia produces two main crops: wheat and olives, a common combination throughout much of the Mediterranean. The region boasts some of the most extensive areas planted with these crops, of which it is one of the leading Italian producers in terms of both quantity and quality.

106 right All roads in Puglia pass cultivated fields, which form a patchwork of colors that changes with the seasons and the various stages of the agricultural cycle. The rows of olives and vines are the most visible from above.

109 In Puglia olive trees surround dazzling white *trulli*, offer shade to noble farmhouses, hide relics of the past, reach the dizzy openings of caves and ravines, guard manors and castles, look out over the sea among Mediterranean perfumes, and penetrate the valleys of the Gargano peninsula, the rocks of the Murge and the Serre Salentine hills.

ing a reconnaissance flight. The excavations, commenced by the officer in 1949 and still far from complete, have uncovered an area of 32,300 sq. ft (3000 sq. m) that accounts for just 1 percent of the entire settlement, where Mother Earth was worshipped in prehistoric times. In addition to the outer ditches, the most important discoveries are more than 100 small C-shaped ditches that enclosed the individual houses, and other everyday structures such as circular wells for drawing water and silos for storing food supplies.

Puglia is not all flat land, however, for it is also home to mountains, such as Monte Gargano, a natural haven with great biodiversity. The mountain of the archangel Michael, miracles and, more recently, Saint Pio of Pietralcina, it is a unique nature reserve whose isolation makes it home to an incredible variety of fauna and particularly flora. The peninsula is formed by rounded mountains never more than 3330 ft (1005 m) high. They are characterized by breathtaking deep canyons eroded by the action of ancient rivers and the wind; surface and underground karst formations with hundreds of sinkholes and chasms; and many different plant habitats and ecosystems that allow an extraordinary variety of life forms. There are over 2000 plant species alone – equivalent to 35 percent of the entire Italian flora (approximately 6000 recorded species) – the most numerous of which are wild orchids, with several dozen species. The promontory is partly covered by the remains of the majestic Umbra Forest, its untamed heart, where life follows a slow,

110 left and center The olive tree is the symbol of the landscape and rural life of Puglia, which is home to 50 million specimens. Its precious fruits make it a veritable goldmine, for they yield high-quality oil with superior sensory characteristics that is widely used in the local cuisine to enhance all kinds of dishes, particularly those made of wild vegetables.

forgotten pace. This "Cathedral of Creation, where even the trees pray," as St Pio described it, is a blanket of monumental beeches that was known to the ancient Romans as the Nemus Garganicum. The shady forest covers 58 sq. miles (150 sq. km) of wild land, where the sun creates plays of light between the leaves. In 1995 it was incorporated into a national park covering a total area of over 470 sq. miles acres (1217 sq. km), which also protects the Gargano's historical, artistic and archaeological heritage. The entire area is teeming with stone relics of the past, dating from prehistoric times to the fervidly religious Middle Ages: the abbey of Monte Sacro, the hermitages of Pulsano, the solitary Castelpagano, the prehistoric rock paintings of Paglicci cave, the dry-stone barns and the procession of shrines along the Via Sacra Langobardorum leading to the cave of San Michele in the picturesque little town of Monte Sant'Angelo.

The best way to leave the promontory is across the arid Gargano steppe, which extends as far as the eye can see to the Daunian Apennines on the horizon. These mountains are crossed by the Via Traiana and their slopes are covered with ancient woods of beech and oak. The valleys are home to fast-flowing streams, waterfalls, blue lakes and the favorite green pastures of shepherds, who make tasty cheese and unique charcuterie products, such as the famed Faeto ham. This part of Puglia was ruled by the Romans, Byzantines, Lombards, Swabians and Angevins, who built bridges, fortified farmhouses, castles, watchtowers, manors, and palaces.

Farther south, beyond the Ofanto valley and the Fossa Bradanica, lies the Murge plateau. This wild, rugged mountainous region is swept by winds that flatten the asphodels, ferulas, low-growing mastic shrubs and strawberry trees on which lesser kestrels perch. Limestone is omnipresent here and everything is recorded in the rock, commencing with the area's geological history, many millions of years old. The huge plateau, protected by the Alta Murgia National Park since 2004, is riddled with deep chasms (known as *gravi*) and sinkholes, whose spectacular sheer walls plunge hundreds of feet into the earth. There are also numerous sharply defined karst valleys *(lame)* in which multicolored orchids grow. Thousands of dinosaur footprints are clearly visible in the Pontrelli quarry in Altamura, while the fossil remains of the ancient Altamura Man can be seen among striking alabaster formations in the Lamalunga cave. The landscape is marked by the age-old signs of sheep farming and transhumance: dry-stone walls that follow the sheep tracks for miles and miles, tower-like *casedde*, similar to the *nuraghi* of Sardinia, and sheep pens, known as *jazzi*. However, there are also the castles and fortresses built by the Nor-

110 right The forests of age-old olive trees are interspersed with wide expanses of wheat and other cereal crops, which reveal the stripes of summer reaping when viewed from above.

mans, Swabians and Angevins. The best known is certainly the octagonal Castel del Monte, the most daring and sublime of the works commissioned by Frederick II in Puglia. Listed by UNESCO as a World Heritage Site, this architectural gem is a stone crown combining Roman, Arab, Norman and Gothic elements, as though the building itself were the eternal expression of the emperor's wide-ranging culture.

Even farther south, the Murge plateau is characterized by cultivated fields wrenched from the rock by the laborious and self-sacrificing peasants described by the regional writer Tommaso Fiore (1884-1973) as the "ants of Puglia." It is dotted with clusters of trulli, farmhouses resembling fortified strongholds and Marian shrines built from limestone slabs. Beneath the ground, hundreds of caverns are adorned with stalactites and stalagmites formed by the slow dripping of water. Examples include the caves of Castellana Grotte, the Trullo cave in Putignano and the Nove Casedde cave in Martina Franca near the Pianelle forest. The Messapian plain covers the ancient province of Terra d'Otranto, while the inland areas of the modern provinces of Taranto, Brindisi and Lecce form the Salentine Peninsula. From the sky, it all appears as a huge expanse of green and silver, a sea of olive groves, composed of mysterious, ancient, twisted trees. A thousand natural and historical itineraries can be followed in this land of extra-virgin oil, starting with the shady oak forests that blend into carpets of scrub ending in breathtaking sheer drops. Below, the ravines are one of the most important geological and natural monuments of Southern Italy. These rugged karst features were ennobled during the 9th and 10th centuries by the Basilian monks of the Orthodox Church who used the caverns to house their lavras and crypts, which are decorated with remarkable Byzantine frescoes. The finest of these underground art galleries of medieval rock painting can be found in the ravines of Ginosa, Castellaneta, Laterza, Mottola, Massafra, Crispiano, Grottaglie and Statte. Numerous fortified farmhouses appear like the beads of a rosary from above, scattered everywhere and flanked by dovecotes. Their oil mills, where men and animals labored long hours to crush the olives, are often housed below ground.

Many ancient megalithic monuments such as dolmens, menhirs and specchie (heaps of dry stones) can be seen around Calimera, Minervino di Lecce and Guardignano in the province of Lecce. There are also Marian shrines, well hidden among the fertile olive groves. One of the finest is Santa Maria delle Cerrate in Squinzano. Everything in these areas grows and flourishes, including the arts. The Baroque architecture of Lecce is an extraordinary example that can be admired in the towns and cities of Italy's heel.

113 From the Gargano to the Salentine Peninsula, Puglia's vineyards are undergoing great expansion. The region is a sort of Bacchic paradise, where great DOC wines are produced, and an oasis for table grapes, which are also grown under glass, making the region one of the leading European exporters of the fruit.

114 The laboriousness of the peasants of the southern Murge plateau can be read in the strange geometric patches of fertile red earth, wrenched from the rugged limestone rock and bounded by dry-stone walls.

115 Age-old olive trees are not the only features of the Murge plateau and Salentine Peninsula, which are also home to large fields planted with wheat and other cereal crops. Pictures like this are a common sight in summer, when reaping and the successive plowing create bizarre patterns on the ground, watched over by silent stands of olive trees.

116 and 117 The great Italian poet and writer Giuseppe Ungaretti sang the praises of the sunny Apulian Tableland in *Il deserto e dopo*: ". . . here too is the realm of the true sun, the raging sun. You can feel it from the cloud of dust, as soon as you take a couple of steps outside. I nostalgically think that it must be an unprecedented spectacle to see it here in summer, at its finest hour, as it transforms the stone into the flickering of fragments at the height of its strength. There is no rivulet nor tree. The plain opens like a sea. I would like to see it here unleashing its full power, rippling in the agonizing breath of the west wind, above the crazed wheat. It is my sun, the creator of solitude; and, in it, the wandering bleating of this time of year make its infinity too crepuscular; barely marred by the road to the sea. And at night, once again the sheep alone will move the clouds, amassed beneath the portico of a remote farmhouse."

118 and 119 Lucera (Foggia province) boasts an array of historic monuments that justifies a visit to the town at any time of year. The most interesting ones include the castle where Frederick II interned the Sicilian Arabs and the oval Roman amphitheater, built in the 1st century B.C. by Marcus Vecilius Campus in honor of Emperor Augusuts.

120 An Italian national monument since 1876 and a UNESCO World Heritage Site, the extraordinary octagonal Castel del Monte, in the municipality of Andria, was built in 1240, with octagonal towers at each corner.

121 The perfectly octagonal Castel del Monte is shaded by a wood on top of a hill, 1770 feet above sea level, and can be seen from the Murge plateau to the Gargano peninsula, the Ofanto and Bradano valleys, the Vulture area and the Irpinia hills.

123 An isolated farmhouse at the center of an estate, the blazing sun and crops aligned in geometric patterns with striking color contrasts form a typical picture-postcard view of the Salentine Peninsula, a land with great agricultural and peasant traditions.

124

124-125 Vineyards and fields planted with cereals are dotted all over the region that stretches from the Gargano to the Salentine Peninsula. This part of Italy is blessed with the ideal geological and climatic conditions for these crops and is rightly considered the breadbasket of Italy.

126 The countryside around Alberobello (Bari province) mirrors the intriguing town, for it is covered with dirt tracks leading to unexpected farmhouses and dotted with *trulli*, like a little village where time seems to have stood still or followed other rhythms.

127 left and right The Itria valley is a huge sunny garden created over the centuries by the laborious peasants whom the writer Tommaso Fiore (1884-1973) described as the "ants of Puglia." All the stones have been piled into dry-stone walls, miles long, and magnificent *trulli*, resembling fairytale houses, where it has become a luxury to live – particularly in the urban triangle on the borders between three provinces, comprised within the municipal territory of the towns of Martina Franca (Taranto province), Locorotondo (Bari province) and Cisternino (Brindisi province).

128 and 129 The gleaming ruins of Gnathia – founded by the Messapii, and a Roman
municipium from the 3rd century B.C. – lie between Torre Canne and Monopoli on the Adriatic
coast, on the border between the provinces of Bari and Brindisi. Visitors can admire the city's
walls, acropolis, ancient port and lower city, with houses, workshops, forum, kilns, tombs and two
Early Christian basilicas. Excavations have yielded archaeological finds including the famous
vases of Gnathia, dating from the 3rd-4th centuries B.C., now housed in the National
Archaeological Museum behind the partly buried city.

130 The flat countryside of the Salentine Peninsula becomes lush green in spring, setting off the cubic architecture of houses and towers painted in pastel hues mellowed by the sun and the years. Each house has its own driveway that ends in a courtyard, usually paved with stone, where wheat was once threshed after reaping and olives were loaded onto carts to be taken to the oil mills.

131 Farmhouses are the symbols of country life in Puglia. The region's vast expanses are dotted with hundreds of these buildings, which can be divided into four types: with a tower, fortified without a tower, castle-shaped, and non-fortified *da pecore e da campo* ("for sheep and crops") with adjoining trulli or barns.

132 In spring the soft forms of the wide Bradano river valley, known as the Fossa Bradanica, on the border with Basilicata, resemble a green carpet, dotted here and there with little farmhouses and streaked along the course of the streams with the remains of the original tree cover that once extended over the entire area.

133 The paths running along the coast near Polignano a Mare (Bari province) form geometric patterns around the fields, dotted here and there with *trulli* and farmhouses.

134-135 Like in Margherita di Savoia, the saltpans in Zapponeta, near Foggia, form an evocative puzzle of pools, tanks, drainage pumps, channels, locks, banks and heaps of salt crystals, which were once gathered by hand by the saltworkers, but are now transported by conveyor belts.

137 A farmhouse dominates the stretch of coast between Monopoli (Bari province) and Polignano a Mare. The surrounding fields are marked with dry-stone walls, locally known as *gisure* (or *cisure*).

138 and 139 The Apulian countryside (these three views show various aspects of the inland area of Taranto province) is mainly flat, with medium-sized hills only on the central Murge plateau. The Murge Tarantine is a flat, low-lying area, well suited for growing vines and olive trees.

140-141 Puglia is one of the most agriculturally productive areas of Italy, as demonstrated by this view showing fields extending as far as the eye can see. With over 50 million olive trees and countless vines, Puglia is the leading producer of olive oil and table grapes, with a cultivated area of over 1875 sq. miles (4856 sq. km), and second in production of wheat and oats.

COASTS AND ISLANDS

Puglia is a region with an amazing 500 miles (805 km) of coast. It offers countless seascapes and splendid bird's-eye views, starting with the Tremiti Islands, the only archipelago belonging to the region. Although small, they have many interesting sights and stories. The islands of San Domino, San Nicola, Cretaccio, Capraia and Pianosa are home to a protected marine reserve, with crystal-clear sea brimming with life. They are the setting for tales of fishermen and legends like that of the mythical hero Diomedes. They were also at the center of events featuring Benedictine and Cistercian monks, pirates, exiles from the Kingdom of Naples and opponents of Fascism. The fortified island of San Nicola, dominated by the Renaissance façade of the church of Santa Maria a Mare, is home to a series of monuments and pine trees on the rocky coast overlooking cliffs and grottoes. The Gargano Peninsula is visible beyond, across the sea. The boundaries of the national park extend as far as the coastal lakes on the northern side of the promontory, which are the largest in Italy. Lesina and Varano are dazzling at all times of day, but the best moment to admire them from above – perhaps from the limestone heights of Monte d'Elio – is at sunset, when the water is flushed a deep red and the lakes resemble the craters of twin volcanoes. Resident and migratory birds, eels, scrubland and coastal dunes make them the ideal destinations for nature lovers. Torre Mileto is situated slightly farther east, where the low coast starts to rise into rocks and cliffs on which the maze-like Vuccolo quarter of Rodi Garganico is perched. The rugged cliffs then give way to long sandy beaches backed by luxuriant pine groves before suddenly rising again after Calenella until reaching Peschici, dominated by the Norman fortress. The old town is an intricate maze of narrow streets that wind among the churches and white houses.

From this point onward the coast forms a long series of bays and coves guarded by watchtowers and ingenious *trabucchi* (fishing machines) on tiny headlands: San Nicola, Calalunga, Usmai, Sfinale, Porticello. It is also home to important archaeological sites, including the La Salata necropolis used between the 4th and 6th

142 left State Highway 16 runs along the entire length of Puglia's Adriatic coast, connecting some of the region's most representative landscapes and cities. Here the road winds near Monopoli, south of Bari.

142 right A lighthouse dominates Punta della Provvidenza, the southernmost tip of San Domino (Tremiti Islands, Foggia province), beyond the pine grove of the same name that covers the highest point of the island (380 ft/116 m). Slightly farther west, the entrance of the Bue Marino grotto can be seen at the foot of a towering cliff.

143 The sea is one of Puglia's natural resources. The limestone rocks near Vieste offer breathtaking sights such as that depicted here.

145 North of Otranto (Lecce propvince), before the Almini coastal lakes, the Adriatic is bordered by highly stratified cliffs and dotted with stacks. The most breathtaking spectacle is at dawn, when the rock is flushed with fiery colors.

centuries B.C.; the Defensola prehistoric mine; and the grotto and Bronze Age necropolis at Punta Manaccora. Vieste is particularly beautiful from above, because it extends along a limestone crest to Punta San Francesco, with the little church of the same name and a *trabucco* perched above the sea. The old town is full of surprises: Piazzetta le Ripe, the 11th-century Romanesque cathedral of Santa Maria di Merino and the Norman castle, built in 1240 to scan the horizon for pirates and protect the city from them. A long stretch of sand extends from the famous Pizzomunno monolith, and is followed by Gattarella tower, the picturesque arch of San Felice, the bay of Campi, and Pugnochiuso, with aromatic scrubland and unbelievably transparent waters. The flint-streaked white cliffs fall most spectacularly in-

to the sea at Vignanotica, behind the bay of Zagare with the Mergoli rocks, and at Monte Saraceno with its Daunian necropolis. Mattinata, at the foot of this mountain, stands on a plain of olive groves and is, not surprisingly, an important oil production center. On the other side of the Gravaglione Pass lies Manfredonia, named after Manfred of Sicily, the son of Frederick II, which boasts a massive castle. The town is also home to the handsome Apulian Romanesque churches of Santa Maria di Siponto and San Leonardo, which vaunts the finest sculpted portal of the entire region. The shallow waters of Lake Salso and the pink saltpans of Margherita of Savoia are the best spots to admire the Gargano Peninsula from a distance, from which it resembles an island. The rest of the coast is sandy, with a few rocky out-

146 left Perfumed green crowns loom over the white cliffs on the coast at Vieste (Foggia province) as it races toward Mattinata. The Aleppo pine woods are one of the natural wonders of the Gargano National Park.

crops on which important medieval towns were built in Apulian Romanesque style under Norman and Swabian rule. The culmination of this architectural style can be seen between Barletta and Giovinazzo in the cathedrals that rise above the fishing villages. Barletta, the scene of the famous Challenge between Ettore Fieramosca and Charles de la Motte, is home to the cathedral of Santa Maria Maggiore near the bronze statue known as the Colossus (4th century A.D.). The cathedral of San Nicola Pellegrino in Trani was founded in 1097 on two crypts on different levels (that of San Nicola and the hypogeum of San Leucio). It has a 200-ft (61 m) bell tower and a smooth façade interrupted only by a rose window and a portal decorated with sculpted animal and plant figures. Farther along the coast, beyond the olive groves surrounding the Placa dolmen, other examples of Romanesque architecture include the cathedral of San Pietro in the old town of Bisceglie, the picturesque cathedral of San Carlo in Molfetta, with its tall bell towers overlooking the port, and the cathedral of Giovinazzo, where the Crusaders bound for the Holy Land used to stop to pray.

In the southern part of the province of Bari, beyond Mola, the coast is wilder and rockier, with little fjords and reefs, submerged grottoes and caves. This stretch commences with the bay of Torre Incina and the fishing village of San Vito, with its 9th-century fortified monastery, followed by the sheer cliffs of Lama Monachile, just north of Polignano a Mare, the birthplace of Domenico Modugno. The little town is full of narrow streets that wind their way between the church of Santa Maria Assunta, Piazza Vittorio Emanuele and the entrances to the Ardito and Palazzese caves. The atmosphere in Monopoli is very similar. Its old town boasts treasures including the rock crypt of the Madonna del Soccorso, the 12th-century Romanesque cathedral of the Madonna della Madia, and a castle with fortified walls. Gnathia, "built against the will of the nymphs," to use the words of Basilicatan poet Orazio Flacco, is our next stop. The walls, acropolis, old port, lower town and Early Christian basilicas of this town founded by the Messapii, and a flourishing Roman *municipium* from the 3rd century B.C., have survived the passage of thousands of years. The coast is backed by olive groves and fortified farmhouses. Torre Coccaro, Torre Maizza, Montalbano, Ottava Piccola, Malzarossa, Maccarone, San Domenico and Lo Spagnuolo are just a few of the sumptuously elegant manors that dot the area as far as the tourist port of Ostuni. This little city is a mass of white houses, palaces, Baroque portals and arches dominated by a Late-Gothic cathedral near Piazza della Libertà with the Baroque obelisk of

146 center The Salentine Peninsula boasts a system of watchtowers that form a defensive chain. The entire coastline is punctuated with these fortified structures built from the 16th century onward to protect the promontory from the attacks of "the Turks, who put ashore in our marinas, sacking several farmhouses. . . ." as a 1714 document recounts.

146 right The Ionian coast of the Salentine Peninsula is less rugged, with tropical-looking white sandy beaches, such as that of Porto Cesareo (Lecce province), which offers views of Conigli island and the other atolls and frames a picturesque little fishing port.

Sant'Oronzo. Toward Brindisi we encounter the Marine Protected Area of Torre Guaceto, and farther south – in the province of Lecce – the pine forest and wetlands of the Le Cesine nature reserve.

There are plenty of other sights to admire along the coast, including the ancient walls of the Messapian town of Roca Vecchia, which stands on a rocky promontory, and the sandy beaches and cliffs of Torre dell'Orso, Sant'Andrea and Alimini, beyond the lakes teeming with life. Then there's Otranto, the legendary city sacked by the Turks in 1480, whose cathedral houses the ossuary of the 800 martyrs, along with the stone mosaic of the tree of life by the monk Pantaleone. The Serpe tower can be glimpsed between the flagged streets and gates of the medieval city, rising silently against the winds of the Adriatic. The same coast is also home to the Sant'Emiliano and Minervino towers, from which the warning *mamma li turchi* ("Mamma, the Turks!") was cried each time a Saracen sail was spied on the horizon, and the bay of Porto Badisco, where Aeneas is said to have landed, close to the entrances of the Grotta dei Cervi cave with its many Neolithic paintings. Santa Cesarea Terme and Porto Miggiano seem to be under a timeless Mediterranean spell, with their Islamic architecture and isolated rocks. The coast here becomes sheer, with towering cliffs riddled with the Romanelli and Zinzulusa caves and the fjord-like Ciolo channel, with its perfumes of myrtle, rosemary and rockrose. The dizzy heights continue as far as Santa Maria di Leuca, on the far tip of Italy's heel. However, once around the cape, which the Romans called Finibus Terrae –the limit of the land – the shore subsides into a series of silent white sandy beaches: Torre Vado, Torre Pali, Torre Mozza and Torre San Giovanni.

The pearl of the Ionian Sea is Gallipoli, whose name is derived from the Greek *Kalépólis*, meaning "Beautiful City." An aerial view clearly reveals the ring shape of the old town, packed with monuments that include a 16th-century castle, palaces with oriental motifs, underground oil mills and Baroque churches. Continuing northward, we pass over Santa Maria al Bagno, the Cenate pine grove with its Moorish- and Art-Nouveau-style villas, and the ancient coast of Porto Selvaggio, whose name (meaning "wild port") reveals its untamed nature. The forest of Aleppo pine mixed with holm oak and scrub hides the entrances to caves that were once inhabited by Neanderthal man. More coastal towers are dotted along the coast of Uluzzu Bay, San Isidoro and Porto Cesareao as far as the tourist ports of San Pietro in Bevagna, Maruggio, Leporano and Pulsano in the province of Taranto. This area has countless long beaches, cane thickets with freshwater springs, submerged relics of classical antiquity, and luxuriant vegetation among the pine groves of the little ports of Castellaneta and Ginosa.

149 Punta Diamante lies at the far northern end of the island of San Domino (Tremiti Islands, Foggia). The photograph shows the Cretaccio rock and the tip of the island of San Nicola, with its port.

150 The Salentine Peninsula's entire coastline is dotted with watchtowers and lighthouses. The first towers were built in the 16th century to guard against the danger of Turkish invasions.

151 The treacherous seabed has caused many shipwrecks along the Puglia coast. The photograph shows the Eden V, which ran aground near Lesina Marina (Foggia province).

152-153 The Gargano peninsula (shown here near Pugnochiuso, Foggia province) is completely separate from the Apennine range. Its mountains reach a height of over 3300 feet (Monte Calvo, Montenero, Monte Spigno and Monte Croce), sometimes sloping gently to the sea, and in other cases falling sheer, as in this photo.

154 The Gargano coast near Vieste (Foggia province) forms a series of coves and bays framed by rugged rocks, such as the famous Mergoli stacks.

155 The cliffs of the Gargano peninsula are authentic marine paradises for tourists and visitors seeking sun and sea.

156 The white monolith known as Pizzomunno rises at the end of Portunuovo beach in Vieste (Foggia province), on the Gargano peninsula. A local legend recounts that the rock was once a young man who was the victim of an impossible love.

157 Several *trabucchi*, the ancient fishing machines of the Gargano area, are suspended above the sea on this rocky headland near Peschici (Foggia province). The wooden poles support a large fishing net that is lowered into the water using a system of hoists.

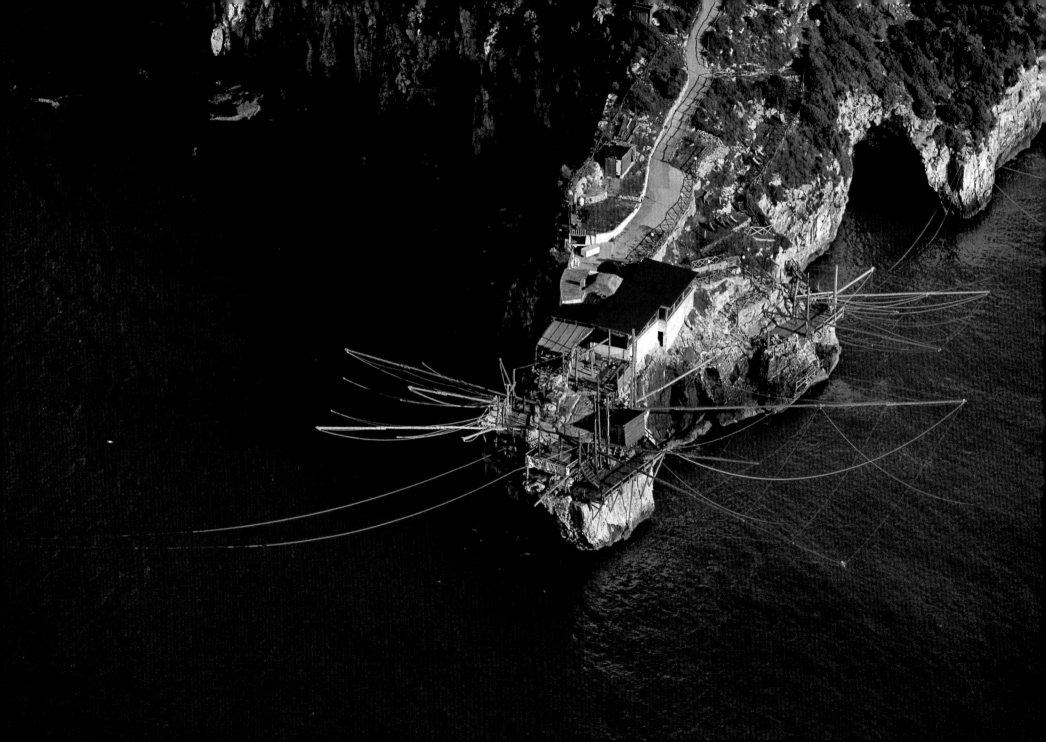

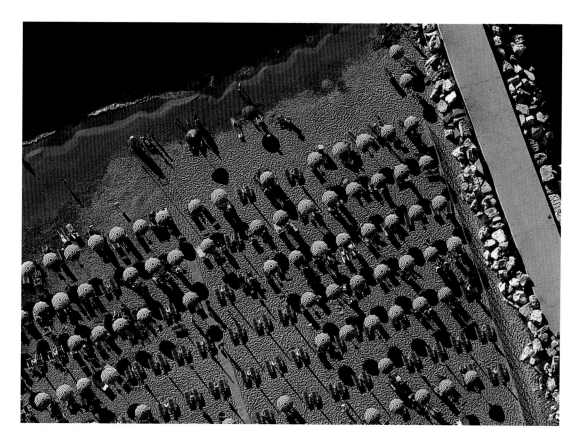

158 and 159 Vieste and Peschici (Foggia province) have beautiful wide golden beaches, perfect for strolling along in all seasons. In summer they are dotted with sun umbrellas and crowded with thousands of holidaymakers.

160-161 The Saline nature reserve in Margherita di Savoia, near Foggia, is home to a wide variety of magnificent birds, including herons, cranes, mute swans and flamingoes.

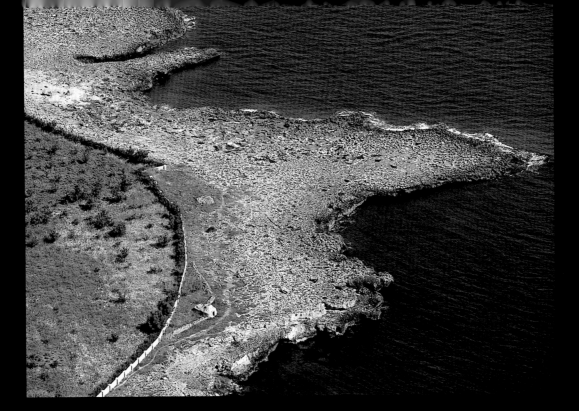

162 The Adriatic coast of the Salentine Peninsula is rocky limestone, which extends to Santa Maria di Leuca (Lecce province). Man has left these rugged lands to nature, enclosing the earthy areas with dry-stone walls and guarding them with barns.

163 Carpets of fertile land surrounded by dirt tracks and dotted with *trulli* shaded by pine or olive trees extend along the Adriatic coast between Mola di Bari and Polignano a Mare.

164 The abbey of Santo Stefano in Monopoli (Bari province) is set like a gem on a low promontory flanked by two white sandy coves, lapped by the crystal-clear sea.

165 Sea, sea and more sea: from mid-spring to early autumn, the local people spend their time on the Ionian or Adriatic coasts. Tourists from all over the world flock to every corner of the region to swim off its wide beaches and stay in its holiday villages with luxuriant gardens.

166 and 167 The numerous coves of the coast around Monopoli (Bari province) are blessed with stunningly clear waters ideal for snorkeling. Many of these spots can be reached only by boat, or along dusty tracks followed by narrow paths and steep steps.

168 The numerous coves of the coast around Monopoli (Bari province) are blessed with stunningly clear waters ideal for snorkeling. Many of these spots can be reached only by boat, or along dusty tracks followed by narrow paths and steep steps.

169 The sand dunes that extend inland from the coast around Brindisi are oases of Mediterranean scrubland. In addition to mastic shrubs, strawberry trees and myrtle, prickly juniper colonizes vast expanses of ancient dunes in an impenetrable tangle of branches that hides mammals such as foxes, weasels and hedgehogs, attracted by the movements of European ratsnakes, green lizards, common toads and tree frogs, or birds such as great tits, blackbirds, blackcaps and robins.

170 The coast north of Brindisi forms a succession of wide bays and sandy beaches. On weekends the city's inhabitants join the tourists on the beaches, which are public as in most of southern Italy.

171 The Torre Guaceto Protected Marine Area and Nature Reserve is a remnant of the huge wetlands that once extended over the Brindisi basin and the Lecce tableland. This fragment saved from drainage covers an area of 5503 acres (22278 hectares) with 5 miles (8 km) of coast between the rocks of Apani and Punta Penna Grossa.

172-173 Cala Sant'Andrea, just south of Roca Vecchia (Lecce province), is worth a visit for its precarious-looking stacks rising a few feet off the coast, which is dotted with rocks and arches that are pummeled by the fury of the waves during the winter.

174 The Le Cesine nature reserve, situated just south of Lecce between San Cataldo and the bays and inlets of Torre Specchia Ruggeri, is an unspoiled corner of the Adriatic where the original wetlands have been preserved and are frequented by many different bird species.

175 and 176-177 The natural beauty of the protected area of the Alimini coastal lakes is a fitting prologue to the monumental and architectural beauty of Otranto (Lecce province). The area boasts thick pine woods that reach down to the sea and endless beaches, lapped by a breathtakingly beautiful sea in which seems a shame not to swim.

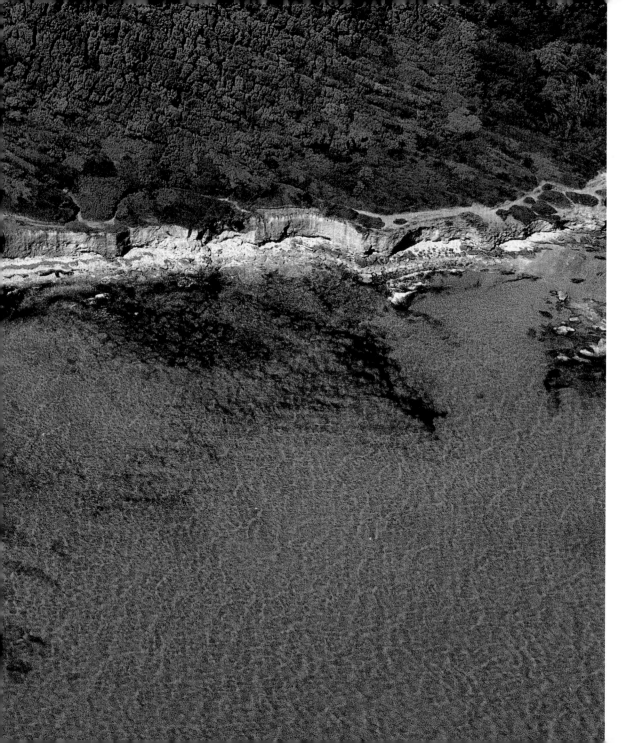

178-179 From the Serre Salentine hills, the limestone descends toward the Adriatic coast near Otranto (Lecce province). However, it does not always do so in the form of bare, sun-baked rock, for it sometimes disappears beneath a green blanket, before reappearing as cliffs on the coast.

180 Visitors to the area around Otranto (Lecce province) should not miss the many coves and little inlets that can be reached by attractive walks among the headily perfumed scrub.

181 During the summer the inhabitants of Lecce head for the nearby beaches of San Cataldo, where the sand and rocks are lapped by clear waters and can be reached along dusty tracks leading off the main roads.

182-183 Near Otranto (Lecce province), the flat landscapes of the inland area of the Salentine Peninsula contrast with the rocky Adriatic coast, which abruptly rises and falls, alternating limestone cliffs with silent beaches.

184 The white lighthouse of the Cape of Otranto looks out over the Adriatic Sea from atop its limestone cliff dotted with the colors of the scrub.

185 Founded during Roman times and restored in 1230 by Frederick II, the Serpe tower is located immediately south of Otranto (Lecce province) of which it is the symbol. It stands on the Cape of Otranto that forms the easternmost tip of the heel of Italy together with Punta Palascia. On clear days it is possible to see the outlines of the mountains of Albania, Epirus and Corfu.

186 The high cliffs forming the southern coast of the Salentine Peninsula dramatically plunge into the Adriatic Sea. They are riddled with large grottoes, such as the Zinzulusa and Romanelli caves (Lecce province).

187 In the southeast the Salentine tableland meets the sea in a curve that forms a little gulf, where the white town of Castro (Lecce province) merges with the Marina, from which many boat trips depart to explore the coast.

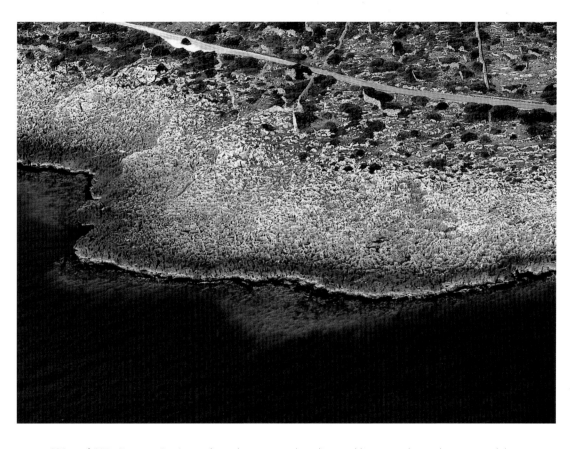

188 and 189 Panoramic views of rare beauty can be glimpsed between the rocky coasts of the marinas of Andrano and Tricase (Lecce province), with towering cliffs where peregrine falcons nest among the dry-stone walls and terraces.

190

190-191 At the tip of the Salentine Peninsula
and the heel of Italy lies a scenic spot called
Capo di Santa Maria di Leuca (Lecce province),
known to the ancient Romans as Finibus Terrae.
It is dominated by a lighthouse and a sanctuary
of the same name that was built on a pagan
temple to Minerva and is said to be an essential
stage in the journey to heaven.

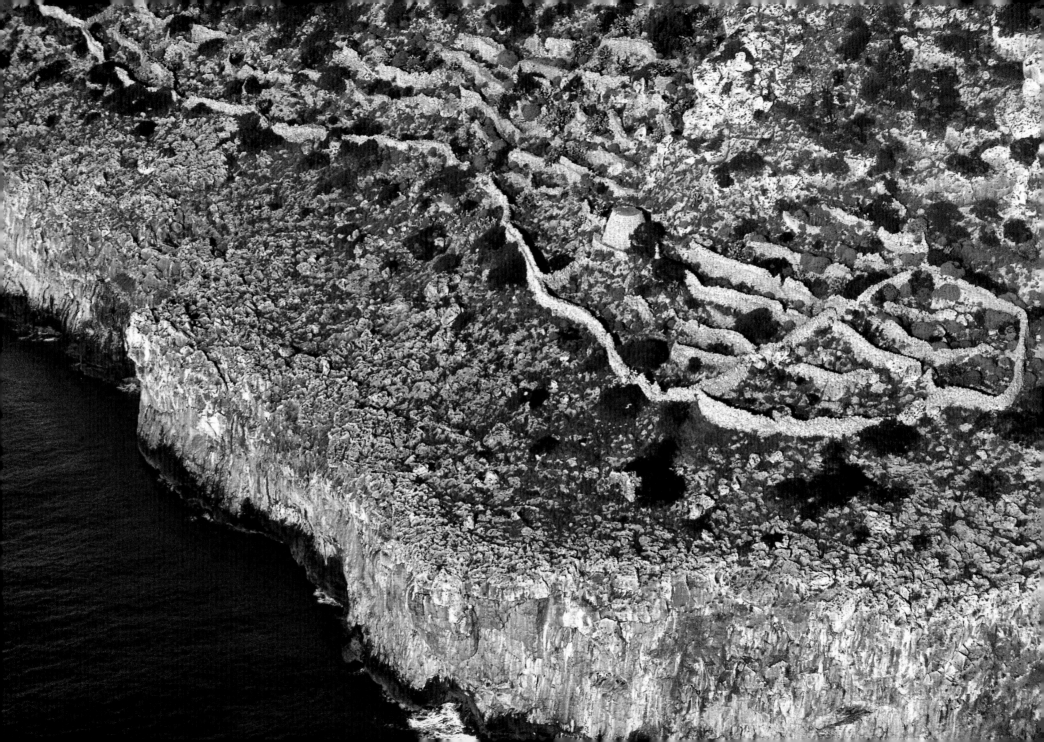

192 The promontory of Santa Maria di Leuca (Lecce province) bears many traces of the ancient agricultural civilization of the Salentine Peninsula, such as *trulli, pagghiare* (large *trulli* with thatched roofs), stone farmhouses and dry-stone walls enclosing the fields.

193 The coast around Marina di Novaglie (Lecce province), not far from the Ciolo channel, is characterized by rocky terrain, baking sun and rugged nature, which man has attempted to tame by terracing and walling the land.

194 Along the coast around Marina di Novaglie (Lecce province), the terraces and walls seem to have adapted themselves to the rugged land like monumental staircases leading down to the sea.

195 The southern Adriatic coast of the Salentine Peninsula has many grottoes accessible only from the sea, such as the huge Zinzulusa cave (Lecce province), full of strangely shaped stalactites resembling rags, known as *zinzuli* in the local dialect. The cavern extends into the limestone, among spectacular mineral formations and underwater tunnels inhabited by a unique and surprising troglobitic fauna.

196-197 The blue expanse of the Ionian Sea is always dotted with many fishing boats that supply the great fish market of Taranto.

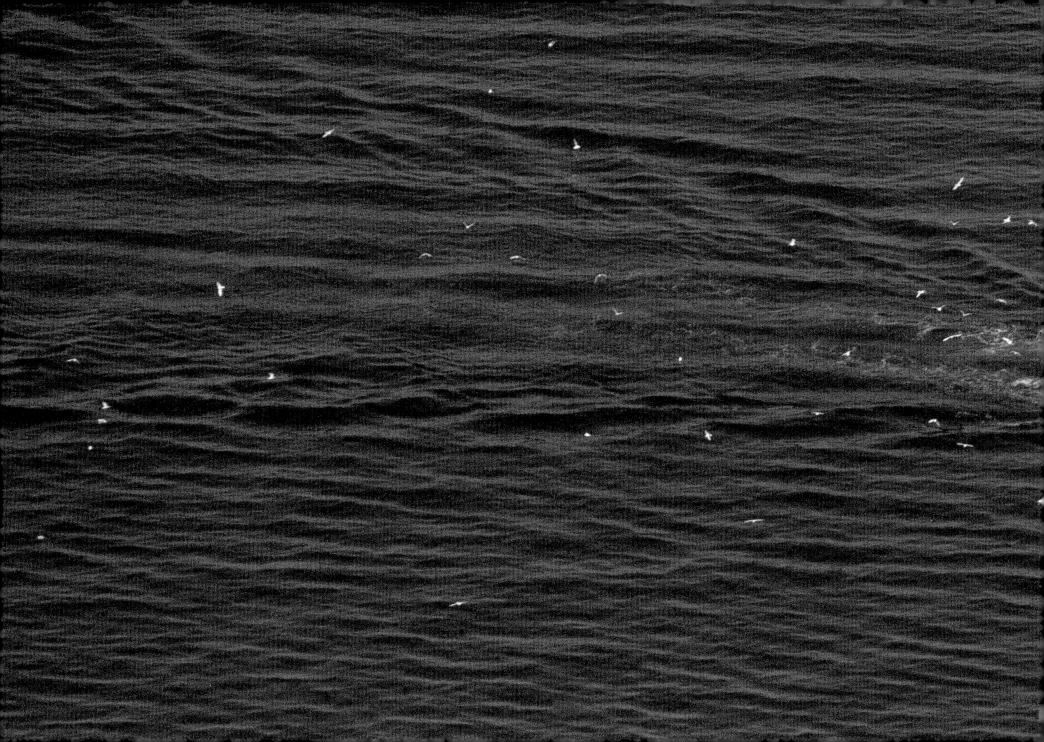

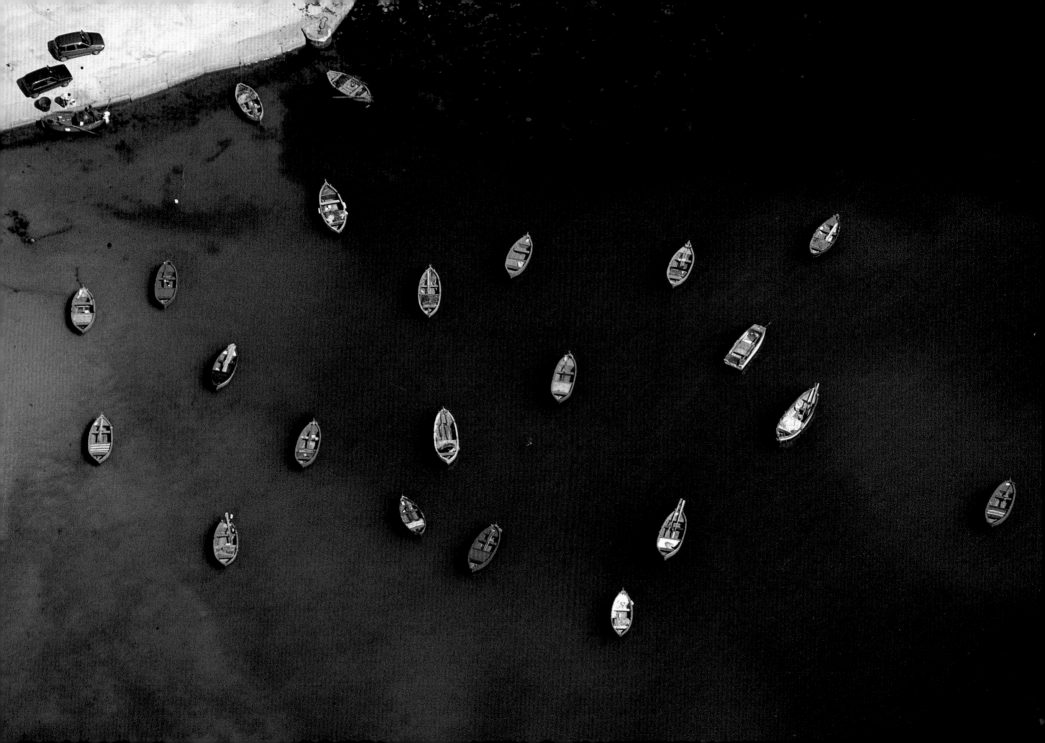

198 Multicolored boats anchored off the Ionian coast near Taranto. Each morning at dawn many fishing boats sail toward the open sea, returning at sunset, according to an age-old tradition.

199 Torre Pali, Torre Vado, Torre Mozza and Torre San Giovanni (Lecce province) are the most exclusive spots of the Ionian coast of the lower Salentine Peninsula, characterized by long golden beaches from which to admire magical sunsets.

201 This rugged stretch of Puglia's Ionian coast conceals a little cove edged with green, low-growing scrub.

202 Porto Selvaggio's name (meaning "Wild Port") reveals its untamed nature. This corner of the Ionian coast of the Salentine Peninsula north of Gallipoli (Lecce province) is home to the park of the same name, which features perfumed woods, sinkholes, troughs and caves brimming with prehistoric traces left by Neanderthal man, as in the Cavallo cave.

203 Crescent-shaped bays and coves enliven the almost completely flat coastline enclosed by prickly juniper between Santa Maria al Bagno, north of Gallipoli, and Taranto.

204-205 The Ionian coast immediately reveals its intentions after rounding Capo di Leuca, where it becomes low and gentle with endless beaches like Marina di Pescoluse, Lido Marini and that of the old Roman port of Usentum.

206 The square tower of Santa Caterina stands on a panoramic hillock among the pine groves and limestone ridges of the Porto Selvaggio nature reserve, offering views of the coast that extend south of Gallipoli.

207 The lighthouse on the island of Sant'Andrea, opposite Gallipoli (Lecce province), was built in 1866 to help fishermen caught in storms. Standing 150 ft (46 m) tall, the lighthouse is built on the flat limestone island that has yielded traces of human occupation dating from the Bronze Age.

208-209 The island of Cretaccio, the smallest of the Tremiti archipelago, lies between San Domino and San Nicola. A visit to San Nicola off season offers a fine chance to discover its old town that, following the legendary foundation of the church of Santa Maria a Mare in the Middle Ages, became a site of pilgrimage and home to a great abbey, controlled in turn by the Benedictines, Cistercians and Lateran Canons Regular.

210 left and right The Tremiti Islands enchant visitors with the incredibly clear waters of the Adriatic Sea, which lap the little ports of San Nicola and San Domino, the tall cliffs and the little ribbons of beaches set between the colored coves.

211 The tour of San Nicola (Tremiti Islands, Foggia province) ends on the bastion of the upper part of the island. The Cavaliere di San Nicolò, clinging to the rock high above the sea, houses a huge circular machicolation with slide for the defense of the narrow Tagliata Passage, which leads to the Asinaro plateau.

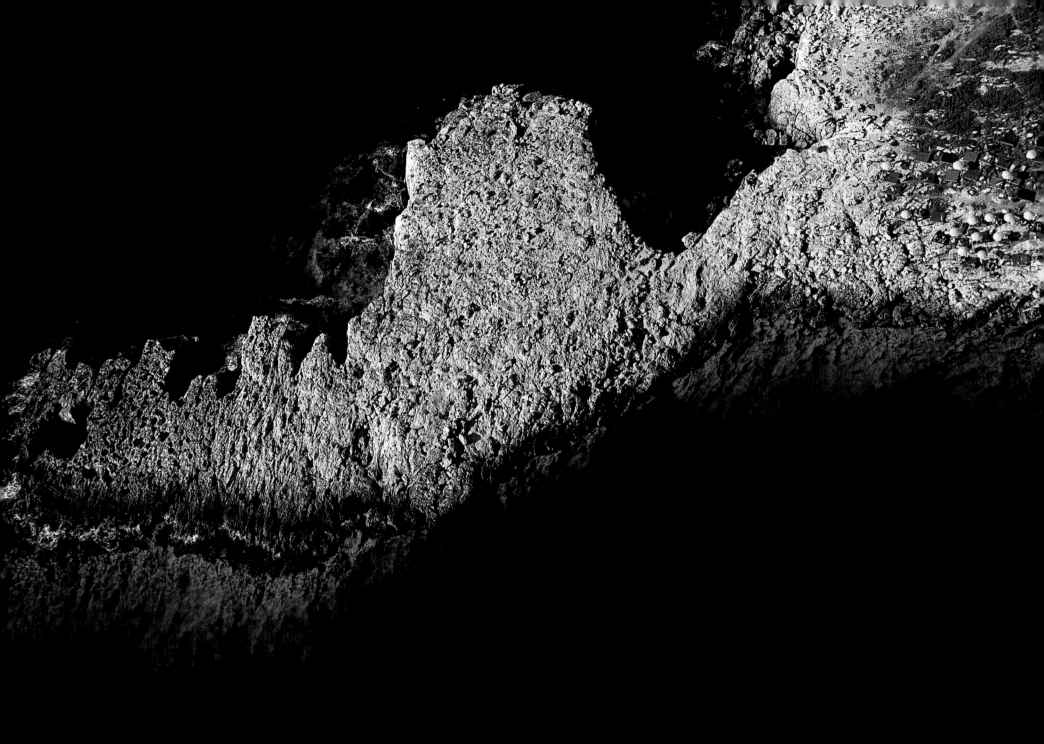

212 Punta del Vucculo on the island of San Domino (Tremiti Islands, Foggia province) extends toward the northwestern shore of the coast before the Tramontana and Tamariello coves, beyond which it forms the triangular Diamante headland.

213 Cala degli Inglesi, on the island of San Domino, is undoubtedly one of the spots with the clearest, cleanest sea of the entire Tremiti archipelago.

214 Punta del Diamante is a spectacular headland on San Domino, the largest of the Tremiti Islands (Foggia province). The thick pinewood that covers the island has earned it the name of "garden of paradise."

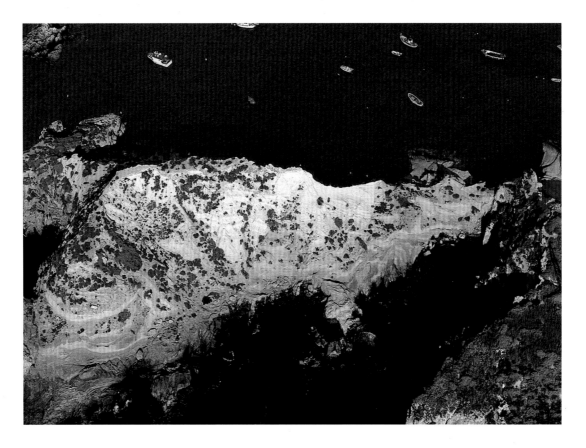

216 San Domino, San Nicola, Cretaccio, Caprara and Pianosa are the names of the Tremiti Islands (Foggia province), which attract thousands of holidaymakers and divers each year. The archipelago is a protected marine area, which also preserves the yellow and gray limestone coast. According to legend, the islands were created by the Homeric hero Diomedes with gigantic stones that he brought from far-off Thrace and threw into the Adriatic after having marked the boundaries of his new homeland, known as Daunia.

217 The western coast of the island of Capraia boasts a series of spectacular bays. The Ottoman galleys took refuge in Cala dei Turchi (shown here) during the attack of 1567.

218 and 219 The Tremiti archipelago is formed by five islands and countless rocks and tiny islets, of which the most famous is that known as the Vecchia. The islands have a resident population of just 420, but are flooded with tourists during the summer, attracted by their untamed nature and spectacular unspoiled sea.

220 The northern coastline of the island of Capraia (Tremiti archipelago) traces a curve with tall cliffs following the sweeping crescent of Cala dei Turchi and, after the lighthouse on Punta del Grottone, forms the limestone finger of Cala Grande and Punta Secca.

Index

Index

Credits:
All photographs are by **Antonio Attini/Archivio White Star** except the following:

Marcello Bertinetti/Archivio White Star: page 31
Alfio Garozzo/Archivio White Star: pages 4-5, 143, 154, 155
Worldsat International Inc.: page 16

Photographs
Antonio Attini

Text
Carlos Solito

Editor
Valeria Manferto De Fabianis
Editorial coordination
Alberto Bertolazzi
Maria Valeria Urbani Grecchi

The publisher would like to thank:
Elio Rullo of Volitalia
Mimmo Potenzieri

© 2008 White Star s.p.a.
Via Candido Sassone, 22/24
13100 Vercelli, Italy
www.whitestar.it

TRANSLATION: SARAH PONTING

ISBN 978-88-544-0370-3

REPRINTS:
1 2 3 4 5 6   12 11 10 09 08

Printed in Cina